MW01242290

This journal belongs

to

_____

STAY
Positive

Think Better Feel Better was designed with the idea of encouraging individuals like you to reset your mindset. I'm sure you've heard this before. But no one ever explains how to go about doing this. This daily journal is structured to help you reprogram your thoughts, set your goals, and maintain a happier healthier you, one day at a time. Within this journal you will break the habit of negative thinking, maintain focus on the bigger picture and you'll be able to see trackable progress. If this sounds like something you're interested in, then this is the right book for you.

FIRST THINGS FIRST
LET'S GET TO KNOW YOU

This is important. Take time to get to know who you are and what may be contributing factors that throw you off day to day. These are the things that keep you from healing and reaching your best self

THINGS THAT MAKE ME HAPPY
(LIST THINGS THAT BRING YOU JOY)

1. ....
2. ....
3. ....
4. ....
5. ....

TRIGGERS
(THINGS THAT CAN CAUSE A NEGATIVE EMOTIONAL REACTION MAKING IT DIFFICULT FOR YOU TO BE PRESENT)

1. ....
2. ....
3. ....
4. ....
5. ....

Monthly Goals

MENTALLY

- ♡ _____
- ♡ _____
- ♡ _____

PHYSICALLY

- ♡ _____
- ♡ _____
- ♡ _____

CAREER

- ♡ _____
- ♡ _____
- ♡ _____

Monthly goals

FINANCES

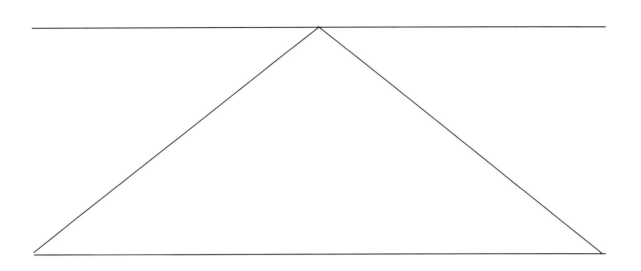

DON'T STOP

· UNTIL YOU'RE PROUD ·

Just *keep going!*

Daily 5 minute journaling

Date _____

_____

_____

_____

_____

_____

_____

_____

_____

_____

_____

_____

_____

_____

_____

_____

_____

_____

_____

_____

Daily check in

DATE _____

WHAT WENT WELL TODAY?
○ _____
○ _____
○ _____

TODAY'S AFFIRMATION

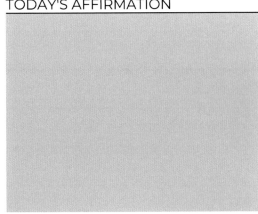

TODAY I FELT

WHAT I WANT TO REMEMBER ABOUT TODAY

WHAT TRIGGERED ME TODAY?

GOALS ACHEIVED TODAY
○ _____
○ _____
○ _____
○ _____

SELF CARE FOR TODAY
EX: MEDITATE FOR 5 MINUTES

MY RANKING OF TODAY

Daily 5 minute journaling

Date _____

_____

_____

_____

_____

_____

_____

_____

_____

_____

_____

_____

_____

_____

_____

_____

_____

_____

_____

Daily check in

DATE _____

WHAT WENT WELL TODAY?

○ _____

○ _____

○ _____

TODAY'S AFFIRMATION

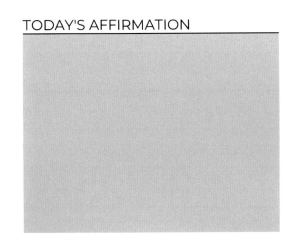

TODAY I FELT

WHAT I WANT TO REMEMBER ABOUT TODAY

WHAT TRIGGERED ME TODAY?

GOALS ACHEIVED TODAY

○ _____

○ _____

○ _____

○ _____

SELF CARE FOR TODAY

EX: MEDITATE FOR 5 MINUTES

MY RANKING OF TODAY

☆ ☆ ☆ ☆ ☆

Daily 5 minute journaling

Date _____

_____

_____

_____

_____

_____

_____

_____

_____

_____

_____

_____

_____

_____

_____

_____

_____

_____

_____

_____

Daily check in

DATE _____

WHAT WENT WELL TODAY?
○ _____
○ _____
○ _____

WHAT TRIGGERED ME TODAY?

TODAY'S AFFIRMATION

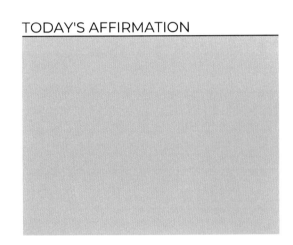

GOALS ACHEIVED TODAY
○ _____
○ _____
○ _____
○ _____

TODAY I FELT

WHAT I WANT TO REMEMBER ABOUT TODAY

SELF CARE FOR TODAY
EX: MEDITATE FOR 5 MINUTES

MY RANKING OF TODAY
☆ ☆ ☆ ☆ ☆

Daily 5 minute journaling

Date _____

_____

_____

_____

_____

_____

_____

_____

_____

_____

_____

_____

_____

_____

_____

_____

_____

_____

_____

_____

Daily check in

DATE _____

WHAT WENT WELL TODAY?
○ _____
○ _____
○ _____

WHAT TRIGGERED ME TODAY?

TODAY'S AFFIRMATION

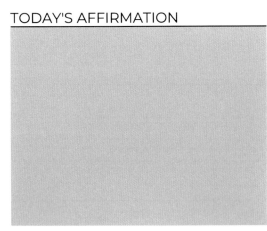

GOALS ACHEIVED TODAY
○ _____
○ _____
○ _____
○ _____

TODAY I FELT

😃 🙂 😐 🙁 😣 😮

WHAT I WANT TO REMEMBER ABOUT TODAY

SELF CARE FOR TODAY
EX: MEDITATE FOR 5 MINUTES

MY RANKING OF TODAY
☆ ☆ ☆ ☆ ☆

Daily 5 minute journaling

Date _____

_____

_____

_____

_____

_____

_____

_____

_____

_____

_____

_____

_____

_____

_____

_____

_____

_____

_____

Daily check in

DATE _____

WHAT WENT WELL TODAY? _____

○ _____

○ _____

○ _____

TODAY'S AFFIRMATION

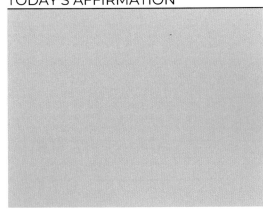

TODAY I FELT

WHAT I WANT TO REMEMBER ABOUT TODAY _____

WHAT TRIGGERED ME TODAY? _____

GOALS ACHEIVED TODAY _____

○ _____

○ _____

○ _____

○ _____

SELF CARE FOR TODAY

EX: MEDITATE FOR 5 MINUTES

MY RANKING OF TODAY _____

Daily 5 minute journaling

Date _____

Daily check in

DATE _____

WHAT WENT WELL TODAY?

○ _____

○ _____

○ _____

WHAT TRIGGERED ME TODAY?

TODAY'S AFFIRMATION

GOALS ACHEIVED TODAY

○ _____

○ _____

○ _____

○ _____

TODAY I FELT

WHAT I WANT TO REMEMBER ABOUT TODAY

SELF CARE FOR TODAY

EX: MEDITATE FOR 5 MINUTES

MY RANKING OF TODAY

☆ ☆ ☆ ☆ ☆

Daily 5 minute journaling

Date _____

_____

_____

_____

_____

_____

_____

_____

_____

_____

_____

_____

_____

_____

_____

_____

_____

_____

_____

_____

Daily check in

DATE _____

WHAT WENT WELL TODAY? _____
- ○ _____
- ○ _____
- ○ _____

TODAY'S AFFIRMATION
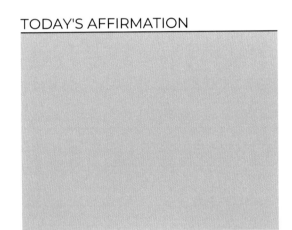

TODAY I FELT

WHAT I WANT TO REMEMBER ABOUT TODAY _____

WHAT TRIGGERED ME TODAY? _____

GOALS ACHEIVED TODAY
- ○ _____
- ○ _____
- ○ _____
- ○ _____

SELF CARE FOR TODAY
EX: MEDITATE FOR 5 MINUTES

MY RANKING OF TODAY
☆ ☆ ☆ ☆ ☆

Daily 5 minute journaling

Date _____

_____

_____

_____

_____

_____

_____

_____

_____

_____

_____

_____

_____

_____

_____

_____

_____

_____

_____

Daily check in

DATE _____

WHAT WENT WELL TODAY?

○ _____

○ _____

○ _____

WHAT TRIGGERED ME TODAY?

TODAY'S AFFIRMATION

GOALS ACHEIVED TODAY

○ _____

○ _____

○ _____

○ _____

TODAY I FELT

WHAT I WANT TO REMEMBER ABOUT TODAY

SELF CARE FOR TODAY

EX: MEDITATE FOR 5 MINUTES

MY RANKING OF TODAY

Daily 5 minute journaling

Date _____

_____

_____

_____

_____

_____

_____

_____

_____

_____

_____

_____

_____

_____

_____

_____

_____

_____

Daily check in

DATE _____

WHAT WENT WELL TODAY?

- ○ _____
- ○ _____
- ○ _____

WHAT TRIGGERED ME TODAY?

TODAY'S AFFIRMATION

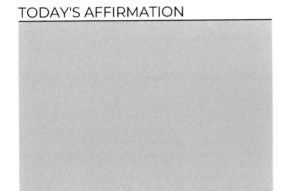

GOALS ACHEIVED TODAY

- ○ _____
- ○ _____
- ○ _____
- ○ _____

TODAY I FELT

SELF CARE FOR TODAY

EX: MEDITATE FOR 5 MINUTES

WHAT I WANT TO REMEMBER ABOUT TODAY

MY RANKING OF TODAY

Daily 5 minute journaling

Date _____

_____

_____

_____

_____

_____

_____

_____

_____

_____

_____

_____

_____

_____

_____

_____

_____

_____

Daily check in

DATE _____

WHAT WENT WELL TODAY?

○ _____

○ _____

○ _____

WHAT TRIGGERED ME TODAY?

TODAY'S AFFIRMATION

GOALS ACHEIVED TODAY

○ _____

○ _____

○ _____

○ _____

TODAY I FELT

SELF CARE FOR TODAY

EX: MEDITATE FOR 5 MINUTES

WHAT I WANT TO REMEMBER ABOUT TODAY

MY RANKING OF TODAY

Daily 5 minute journaling

Date _____

_____
_____
_____
_____
_____
_____
_____
_____
_____
_____
_____
_____
_____
_____
_____
_____
_____
_____
_____

Daily check in

DATE _____

WHAT WENT WELL TODAY?

- ○ _____
- ○ _____
- ○ _____

TODAY'S AFFIRMATION

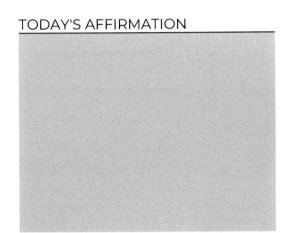

TODAY I FELT

WHAT I WANT TO REMEMBER ABOUT TODAY

WHAT TRIGGERED ME TODAY?

GOALS ACHEIVED TODAY

- ○ _____
- ○ _____
- ○ _____
- ○ _____

SELF CARE FOR TODAY

EX: MEDITATE FOR 5 MINUTES

MY RANKING OF TODAY

☆ ☆ ☆ ☆ ☆

Daily 5 minute journaling

Date _____

_____

_____

_____

_____

_____

_____

_____

_____

_____

_____

_____

_____

_____

_____

_____

_____

_____

Daily check in

DATE _____

WHAT WENT WELL TODAY?
○ _____
○ _____
○ _____

WHAT TRIGGERED ME TODAY?

TODAY'S AFFIRMATION

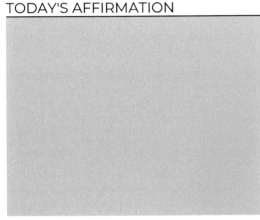

TODAY I FELT

WHAT I WANT TO REMEMBER ABOUT TODAY

GOALS ACHEIVED TODAY
○ _____
○ _____
○ _____
○ _____

SELF CARE FOR TODAY
EX: MEDITATE FOR 5 MINUTES

MY RANKING OF TODAY
☆ ☆ ☆ ☆ ☆

Daily 5 minute journaling

Date _____

_____
_____
_____
_____
_____
_____
_____
_____
_____
_____
_____
_____
_____
_____
_____
_____
_____
_____
_____

Daily check in

DATE _____

WHAT WENT WELL TODAY? _____

○ _____

○ _____

○ _____

WHAT TRIGGERED ME TODAY? _____

TODAY'S AFFIRMATION

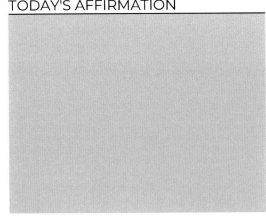

GOALS ACHEIVED TODAY _____

○ _____

○ _____

○ _____

○ _____

TODAY I FELT

SELF CARE FOR TODAY

EX: MEDITATE FOR 5 MINUTES

WHAT I WANT TO REMEMBER ABOUT TODAY _____

MY RANKING OF TODAY _____

    ☆

Daily 5 minute journaling

Date _____

_____

_____

_____

_____

_____

_____

_____

_____

_____

_____

_____

_____

_____

_____

_____

_____

_____

_____

Daily check in

DATE _____

WHAT WENT WELL TODAY?

○ _____

○ _____

○ _____

WHAT TRIGGERED ME TODAY?

TODAY'S AFFIRMATION

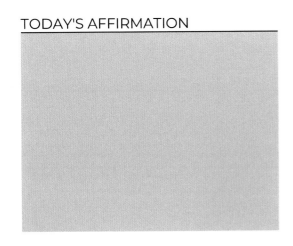

GOALS ACHEIVED TODAY

○ _____

○ _____

○ _____

○ _____

TODAY I FELT

WHAT I WANT TO REMEMBER ABOUT TODAY

SELF CARE FOR TODAY

EX: MEDITATE FOR 5 MINUTES

MY RANKING OF TODAY

☆ ☆ ☆ ☆ ☆

Daily 5 minute journaling

Date _____

_____

_____

_____

_____

_____

_____

_____

_____

_____

_____

_____

_____

_____

_____

_____

_____

_____

_____

Daily check in

DATE _____

WHAT WENT WELL TODAY?

○ _____

○ _____

○ _____

WHAT TRIGGERED ME TODAY?

TODAY'S AFFIRMATION

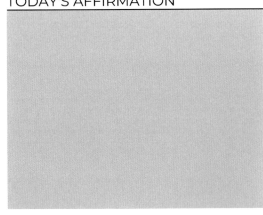

GOALS ACHEIVED TODAY

○ _____

○ _____

○ _____

○ _____

TODAY I FELT

SELF CARE FOR TODAY

EX: MEDITATE FOR 5 MINUTES

WHAT I WANT TO REMEMBER ABOUT TODAY

MY RANKING OF TODAY

☆ ☆ ☆ ☆ ☆

Daily 5 minute journaling

Date _____

_____

_____

_____

_____

_____

_____

_____

_____

_____

_____

_____

_____

_____

_____

_____

_____

_____

_____

Daily check in

DATE _____

WHAT WENT WELL TODAY? _____

○ _____
○ _____
○ _____

WHAT TRIGGERED ME TODAY? _____

TODAY'S AFFIRMATION

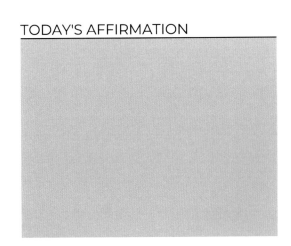

GOALS ACHEIVED TODAY _____

○ _____
○ _____
○ _____
○ _____

TODAY I FELT

SELF CARE FOR TODAY

EX: MEDITATE FOR 5 MINUTES

WHAT I WANT TO REMEMBER
ABOUT TODAY _____

MY RANKING OF TODAY _____

☆ ☆ ☆ ☆ ☆

Daily 5 minute journaling

Date _____

_____

_____

_____

_____

_____

_____

_____

_____

_____

_____

_____

_____

_____

_____

_____

_____

_____

_____

Daily check in

DATE _____

WHAT WENT WELL TODAY?
○ _____
○ _____
○ _____

TODAY'S AFFIRMATION

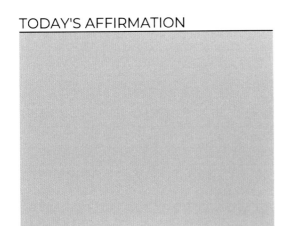

TODAY I FELT

WHAT I WANT TO REMEMBER ABOUT TODAY

WHAT TRIGGERED ME TODAY?

GOALS ACHEIVED TODAY
○ _____
○ _____
○ _____
○ _____

SELF CARE FOR TODAY
EX: MEDITATE FOR 5 MINUTES

MY RANKING OF TODAY
☆ ☆ ☆ ☆ ☆

Daily 5 minute journaling

Date _____

_____

_____

_____

_____

_____

_____

_____

_____

_____

_____

_____

_____

_____

_____

_____

_____

_____

_____

_____

Daily check in

DATE _____

WHAT WENT WELL TODAY? _____

○ _____

_____

○ _____

_____

○ _____

_____

TODAY'S AFFIRMATION

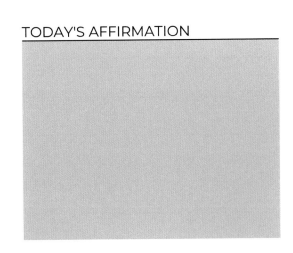

TODAY I FELT

WHAT I WANT TO REMEMBER
ABOUT TODAY _____

WHAT TRIGGERED ME TODAY? _____

GOALS ACHEIVED TODAY _____

○ _____

○ _____

○ _____

○ _____

SELF CARE FOR TODAY
EX: MEDITATE FOR 5 MINUTES

MY RANKING OF TODAY
☆ ☆ ☆ ☆ ☆

Daily 5 minute journaling

Date _____

_____

_____

_____

_____

_____

_____

_____

_____

_____

_____

_____

_____

_____

_____

_____

_____

_____

_____

Daily check in

DATE _____

WHAT WENT WELL TODAY?

○ _____
_____
○ _____
_____
○ _____
_____

WHAT TRIGGERED ME TODAY?

TODAY'S AFFIRMATION

GOALS ACHEIVED TODAY

○ _____
○ _____
○ _____
○ _____

TODAY I FELT

WHAT I WANT TO REMEMBER ABOUT TODAY

SELF CARE FOR TODAY

EX: MEDITATE FOR 5 MINUTES

MY RANKING OF TODAY

Daily 5 minute journaling

Date _____

_____

_____

_____

_____

_____

_____

_____

_____

_____

_____

_____

_____

_____

_____

_____

_____

_____

_____

Daily check in

DATE _____

WHAT WENT WELL TODAY? _____

○ _____

○ _____

○ _____

WHAT TRIGGERED ME TODAY? _____

TODAY'S AFFIRMATION

GOALS ACHEIVED TODAY _____

○ _____

○ _____

○ _____

○ _____

TODAY I FELT

WHAT I WANT TO REMEMBER
ABOUT TODAY _____

SELF CARE FOR TODAY
EX: MEDITATE FOR 5 MINUTES

MY RANKING OF TODAY _____

☆ ☆ ☆ ☆ ☆

Daily 5 minute journaling

Date _____

_____

_____

_____

_____

_____

_____

_____

_____

_____

_____

_____

_____

_____

_____

_____

_____

_____

_____

Daily check in

DATE _____

WHAT WENT WELL TODAY?
- ○ _____
- ○ _____
- ○ _____

TODAY'S AFFIRMATION

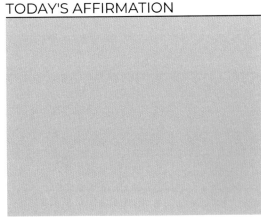

TODAY I FELT

WHAT I WANT TO REMEMBER ABOUT TODAY

WHAT TRIGGERED ME TODAY?

GOALS ACHEIVED TODAY
- ○ _____
- ○ _____
- ○ _____
- ○ _____

SELF CARE FOR TODAY
EX: MEDITATE FOR 5 MINUTES

MY RANKING OF TODAY
☆ ☆ ☆ ☆ ☆

Daily 5 minute journaling

Date _____

Daily check in

DATE _____

WHAT WENT WELL TODAY?

○ _____

○ _____

○ _____

TODAY'S AFFIRMATION

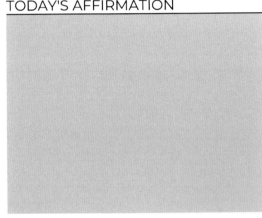

TODAY I FELT

WHAT I WANT TO REMEMBER ABOUT TODAY

WHAT TRIGGERED ME TODAY?

GOALS ACHEIVED TODAY

○ _____

○ _____

○ _____

○ _____

SELF CARE FOR TODAY

EX: MEDITATE FOR 5 MINUTES

MY RANKING OF TODAY

☆ ☆ ☆ ☆ ☆

Daily 5 minute journaling

Date _____

Daily check in

DATE _____

WHAT WENT WELL TODAY?

○ _____

○ _____

○ _____

WHAT TRIGGERED ME TODAY?

TODAY'S AFFIRMATION

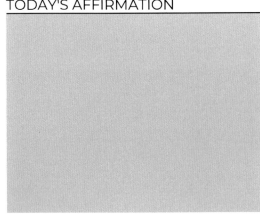

GOALS ACHEIVED TODAY

○ _____

○ _____

○ _____

○ _____

TODAY I FELT

WHAT I WANT TO REMEMBER ABOUT TODAY

SELF CARE FOR TODAY

EX: MEDITATE FOR 5 MINUTES

MY RANKING OF TODAY

☆ ☆ ☆ ☆ ☆

Daily 5 minute journaling

Date _____

_____

_____

_____

_____

_____

_____

_____

_____

_____

_____

_____

_____

_____

_____

_____

_____

_____

Daily check in

DATE _____

WHAT WENT WELL TODAY?
○ _____
_____
○ _____
_____
○ _____
_____

WHAT TRIGGERED ME TODAY?

TODAY'S AFFIRMATION
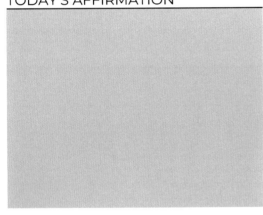

GOALS ACHEIVED TODAY
○ _____
○ _____
○ _____
○ _____

TODAY I FELT

WHAT I WANT TO REMEMBER ABOUT TODAY

SELF CARE FOR TODAY
EX: MEDITATE FOR 5 MINUTES

MY RANKING OF TODAY
☆ ☆ ☆ ☆ ☆

Daily 5 minute journaling

Date _____

_____

_____

_____

_____

_____

_____

_____

_____

_____

_____

_____

_____

_____

_____

_____

_____

_____

_____

Daily check in

DATE _____

WHAT WENT WELL TODAY?

○ _____

○ _____

○ _____

WHAT TRIGGERED ME TODAY?

TODAY'S AFFIRMATION

GOALS ACHEIVED TODAY

○ _____

○ _____

○ _____

○ _____

TODAY I FELT

WHAT I WANT TO REMEMBER ABOUT TODAY

SELF CARE FOR TODAY

EX: MEDITATE FOR 5 MINUTES

MY RANKING OF TODAY

☆ ☆ ☆ ☆ ☆

Daily 5 minute journaling

Date _____

_____
_____
_____
_____
_____
_____
_____
_____
_____
_____
_____
_____
_____
_____
_____
_____
_____

Daily check in

DATE _____

WHAT WENT WELL TODAY?

- ○ _____
- ○ _____
- ○ _____

WHAT TRIGGERED ME TODAY?

TODAY'S AFFIRMATION

GOALS ACHEIVED TODAY

- ○ _____
- ○ _____
- ○ _____
- ○ _____

TODAY I FELT

WHAT I WANT TO REMEMBER ABOUT TODAY

SELF CARE FOR TODAY

EX: MEDITATE FOR 5 MINUTES

MY RANKING OF TODAY

Daily 5 minute journaling

Date _____

Daily check in

DATE _____

WHAT WENT WELL TODAY?

○ _____

○ _____

○ _____

TODAY'S AFFIRMATION

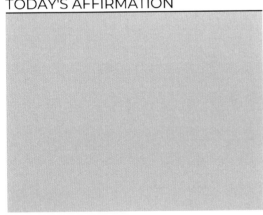

WHAT TRIGGERED ME TODAY?

GOALS ACHEIVED TODAY

○ _____

○ _____

○ _____

○ _____

TODAY I FELT

SELF CARE FOR TODAY

EX: MEDITATE FOR 5 MINUTES

WHAT I WANT TO REMEMBER ABOUT TODAY

MY RANKING OF TODAY

☆ ☆ ☆ ☆ ☆

Daily 5 minute journaling

Date _____

_____

_____

_____

_____

_____

_____

_____

_____

_____

_____

_____

_____

_____

_____

_____

_____

_____

_____

Daily check in

DATE _____

WHAT WENT WELL TODAY? _____

○ _____

○ _____

○ _____

WHAT TRIGGERED ME TODAY?
_____

TODAY'S AFFIRMATION

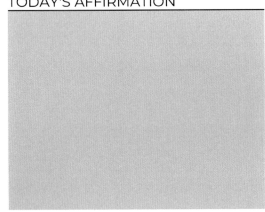

GOALS ACHEIVED TODAY

○ _____

○ _____

○ _____

○ _____

TODAY I FELT

SELF CARE FOR TODAY

EX: MEDITATE FOR 5 MINUTES

WHAT I WANT TO REMEMBER
ABOUT TODAY _____

MY RANKING OF TODAY _____

☆ ☆ ☆ ☆ ☆

Daily 5 *minute journaling*

Date _____

_____

_____

_____

_____

_____

_____

_____

_____

_____

_____

_____

_____

_____

_____

_____

_____

_____

Daily check in

DATE _____

WHAT WENT WELL TODAY?

○ _____

○ _____

○ _____

TODAY'S AFFIRMATION

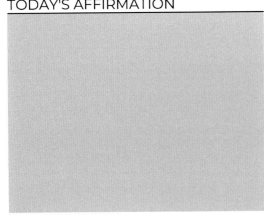

TODAY I FELT

WHAT I WANT TO REMEMBER ABOUT TODAY

WHAT TRIGGERED ME TODAY?

GOALS ACHEIVED TODAY

○ _____

○ _____

○ _____

○ _____

SELF CARE FOR TODAY

EX: MEDITATE FOR 5 MINUTES

MY RANKING OF TODAY

☆ ☆ ☆ ☆ ☆

Daily 5 minute journaling

Date _____

_____

_____

_____

_____

_____

_____

_____

_____

_____

_____

_____

_____

_____

_____

_____

_____

_____

Daily check in

DATE _____

WHAT WENT WELL TODAY? _____

○ _____

○ _____

○ _____

TODAY'S AFFIRMATION

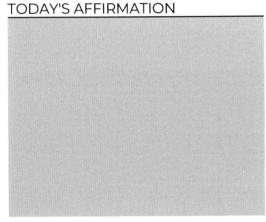

TODAY I FELT

WHAT I WANT TO REMEMBER ABOUT TODAY

WHAT TRIGGERED ME TODAY? _____

GOALS ACHEIVED TODAY _____

○ _____

○ _____

○ _____

○ _____

SELF CARE FOR TODAY
EX: MEDITATE FOR 5 MINUTES

MY RANKING OF TODAY _____

Daily 5 minute journaling

Date _____

_____

_____

_____

_____

_____

_____

_____

_____

_____

_____

_____

_____

_____

_____

_____

_____

_____

_____

Daily check in

DATE _____

WHAT WENT WELL TODAY?
- ○ _____
- ○ _____
- ○ _____

WHAT TRIGGERED ME TODAY?

TODAY'S AFFIRMATION

GOALS ACHEIVED TODAY
- ○ _____
- ○ _____
- ○ _____
- ○ _____

TODAY I FELT

WHAT I WANT TO REMEMBER ABOUT TODAY

SELF CARE FOR TODAY
EX: MEDITATE FOR 5 MINUTES

MY RANKING OF TODAY

Daily 5 minute journaling

Date _____

_____
_____
_____
_____
_____
_____
_____
_____
_____
_____
_____
_____
_____
_____
_____
_____
_____
_____

Daily check in

DATE _____

WHAT WENT WELL TODAY?

○ _____
○ _____
○ _____

WHAT TRIGGERED ME TODAY?

TODAY'S AFFIRMATION

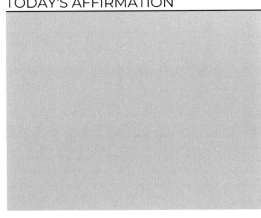

GOALS ACHEIVED TODAY

○ _____
○ _____
○ _____
○ _____

TODAY I FELT

WHAT I WANT TO REMEMBER ABOUT TODAY

SELF CARE FOR TODAY

EX: MEDITATE FOR 5 MINUTES

MY RANKING OF TODAY

☆ ☆ ☆ ☆ ☆

Daily 5 *minute journaling*

Date _____

_____

_____

_____

_____

_____

_____

_____

_____

_____

_____

_____

_____

_____

_____

_____

_____

_____

_____

_____

Daily check in

DATE _____

WHAT WENT WELL TODAY? _____

○ _____

○ _____

○ _____

WHAT TRIGGERED ME TODAY? _____

TODAY'S AFFIRMATION

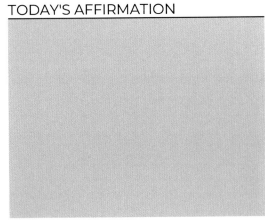

GOALS ACHEIVED TODAY _____

○ _____

○ _____

○ _____

○ _____

TODAY I FELT

WHAT I WANT TO REMEMBER ABOUT TODAY _____

SELF CARE FOR TODAY
EX: MEDITATE FOR 5 MINUTES

MY RANKING OF TODAY _____

☆ ☆ ☆ ☆ ☆

Daily 5 minute journaling

Date _____

Daily check in

DATE _____

WHAT WENT WELL TODAY?
○ _____
○ _____
○ _____

WHAT TRIGGERED ME TODAY?

TODAY'S AFFIRMATION
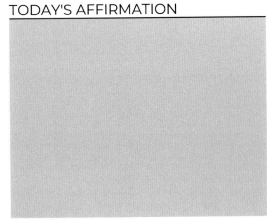

GOALS ACHEIVED TODAY
○ _____
○ _____
○ _____
○ _____

TODAY I FELT

WHAT I WANT TO REMEMBER ABOUT TODAY
_____

SELF CARE FOR TODAY
EX: MEDITATE FOR 5 MINUTES

MY RANKING OF TODAY

Daily 5 minute journaling

Date _____

_____

_____

_____

_____

_____

_____

_____

_____

_____

_____

_____

_____

_____

_____

_____

_____

_____

Daily check in

DATE _____

WHAT WENT WELL TODAY?

○ _____

○ _____

○ _____

WHAT TRIGGERED ME TODAY?

TODAY'S AFFIRMATION

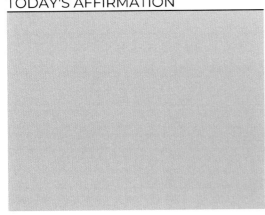

GOALS ACHEIVED TODAY

○ _____

○ _____

○ _____

○ _____

TODAY I FELT

WHAT I WANT TO REMEMBER ABOUT TODAY

SELF CARE FOR TODAY

EX: MEDITATE FOR 5 MINUTES

MY RANKING OF TODAY

☆ ☆ ☆ ☆ ☆

Daily 5 minute journaling

Date _____

_____

_____

_____

_____

_____

_____

_____

_____

_____

_____

_____

_____

_____

_____

_____

_____

_____

_____

_____

Daily check in

DATE _____

WHAT WENT WELL TODAY?

○ _____

○ _____

○ _____

TODAY'S AFFIRMATION

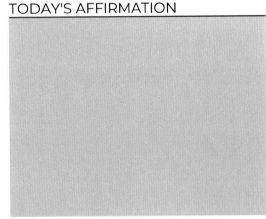

TODAY I FELT

WHAT I WANT TO REMEMBER ABOUT TODAY

WHAT TRIGGERED ME TODAY?

GOALS ACHEIVED TODAY

○ _____

○ _____

○ _____

○ _____

SELF CARE FOR TODAY

EX: MEDITATE FOR 5 MINUTES

MY RANKING OF TODAY

Daily 5 minute journaling

Date _____

Daily check in

DATE _____

WHAT WENT WELL TODAY?

○ _____

○ _____

○ _____

WHAT TRIGGERED ME TODAY?

TODAY'S AFFIRMATION

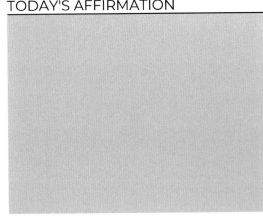

GOALS ACHEIVED TODAY

○ _____

○ _____

○ _____

○ _____

TODAY I FELT

SELF CARE FOR TODAY
EX: MEDITATE FOR 5 MINUTES

WHAT I WANT TO REMEMBER ABOUT TODAY

MY RANKING OF TODAY

Daily 5 minute journaling

Date _____

Daily check in

DATE _____

WHAT WENT WELL TODAY? _____

○ _____

○ _____

○ _____

TODAY'S AFFIRMATION

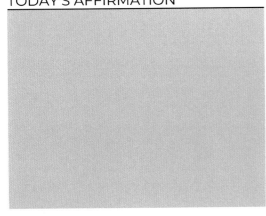

WHAT TRIGGERED ME TODAY? _____

GOALS ACHEIVED TODAY _____

○ _____

○ _____

○ _____

○ _____

TODAY I FELT

SELF CARE FOR TODAY

EX: MEDITATE FOR 5 MINUTES

WHAT I WANT TO REMEMBER ABOUT TODAY _____

MY RANKING OF TODAY

☆ ☆ ☆ ☆ ☆

Daily 5 minute journaling

Date _____

Daily check in

DATE _____

WHAT WENT WELL TODAY?

○ _____

○ _____

○ _____

TODAY'S AFFIRMATION

TODAY I FELT

WHAT I WANT TO REMEMBER ABOUT TODAY

WHAT TRIGGERED ME TODAY?

GOALS ACHEIVED TODAY

○ _____

○ _____

○ _____

○ _____

SELF CARE FOR TODAY

EX: MEDITATE FOR 5 MINUTES

MY RANKING OF TODAY

☆ ☆ ☆ ☆ ☆

Daily 5 minute journaling

Date _____

_____

_____

_____

_____

_____

_____

_____

_____

_____

_____

_____

_____

_____

_____

_____

_____

_____

Daily check in

DATE _____

WHAT WENT WELL TODAY? _____

- ○ _____
- ○ _____
- ○ _____

WHAT TRIGGERED ME TODAY? ____

TODAY'S AFFIRMATION

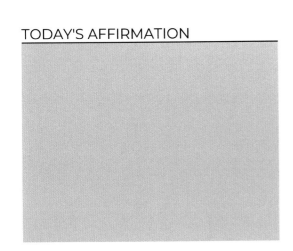

GOALS ACHEIVED TODAY _____

- ○ _____
- ○ _____
- ○ _____
- ○ _____

TODAY I FELT

SELF CARE FOR TODAY

EX: MEDITATE FOR 5 MINUTES

WHAT I WANT TO REMEMBER ABOUT TODAY _____

MY RANKING OF TODAY _____

☆ ☆ ☆ ☆ ☆

Daily 5 minute journaling

Date _____

_____

_____

_____

_____

_____

_____

_____

_____

_____

_____

_____

_____

_____

_____

_____

_____

_____

_____

Daily check in

DATE _____

WHAT WENT WELL TODAY? _____

- ○ _____
- ○ _____
- ○ _____

WHAT TRIGGERED ME TODAY? _____

TODAY'S AFFIRMATION

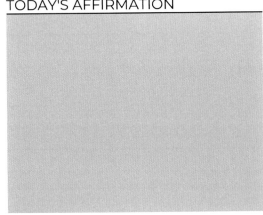

GOALS ACHEIVED TODAY _____

- ○ _____
- ○ _____
- ○ _____
- ○ _____

TODAY I FELT

SELF CARE FOR TODAY

EX: MEDITATE FOR 5 MINUTES

WHAT I WANT TO REMEMBER ABOUT TODAY _____

MY RANKING OF TODAY _____

Daily 5 minute journaling

Date _____

Daily check in

DATE _____

WHAT WENT WELL TODAY? _____

○ _____
○ _____
○ _____

WHAT TRIGGERED ME TODAY? ___

TODAY'S AFFIRMATION

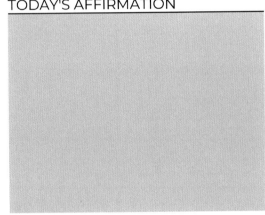

GOALS ACHEIVED TODAY

○ _____
○ _____
○ _____
○ _____

TODAY I FELT

WHAT I WANT TO REMEMBER ABOUT TODAY _____

SELF CARE FOR TODAY

EX: MEDITATE FOR 5 MINUTES

MY RANKING OF TODAY

☆ ☆ ☆ ☆ ☆

Daily 5 minute journaling

Date _____

_____

_____

_____

_____

_____

_____

_____

_____

_____

_____

_____

_____

_____

_____

_____

_____

_____

_____

Daily check in

DATE _____

WHAT WENT WELL TODAY? _____

○ _____

○ _____

○ _____

WHAT TRIGGERED ME TODAY? _____

TODAY'S AFFIRMATION

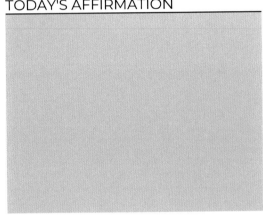

GOALS ACHEIVED TODAY _____

○ _____

○ _____

○ _____

○ _____

TODAY I FELT

WHAT I WANT TO REMEMBER ABOUT TODAY _____

SELF CARE FOR TODAY _____
EX: MEDITATE FOR 5 MINUTES

MY RANKING OF TODAY _____

Daily 5 minute journaling

Date _____

Daily check in

DATE _____

WHAT WENT WELL TODAY?

○ _____

○ _____

○ _____

TODAY'S AFFIRMATION

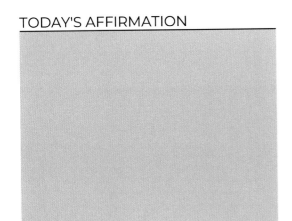

TODAY I FELT

WHAT I WANT TO REMEMBER ABOUT TODAY

WHAT TRIGGERED ME TODAY?

GOALS ACHEIVED TODAY

○ _____

○ _____

○ _____

○ _____

SELF CARE FOR TODAY

EX: MEDITATE FOR 5 MINUTES

MY RANKING OF TODAY

☆ ☆ ☆ ☆ ☆

Daily 5 minute journaling

Date _____

_____
_____
_____
_____
_____
_____
_____
_____
_____
_____
_____
_____
_____
_____
_____
_____
_____
_____

Daily check in

DATE _____

WHAT WENT WELL TODAY?

○ _____

_____

○ _____

_____

○ _____

_____

WHAT TRIGGERED ME TODAY?

TODAY'S AFFIRMATION

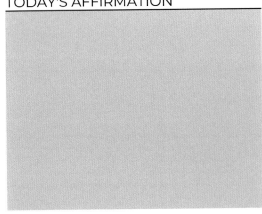

GOALS ACHEIVED TODAY

○ _____

○ _____

○ _____

○ _____

TODAY I FELT

WHAT I WANT TO REMEMBER ABOUT TODAY

SELF CARE FOR TODAY

EX: MEDITATE FOR 5 MINUTES

MY RANKING OF TODAY

Daily 5 minute journaling

Date _____

_____

_____

_____

_____

_____

_____

_____

_____

_____

_____

_____

_____

_____

_____

_____

_____

_____

Daily check in

DATE _____

WHAT WENT WELL TODAY?

○ _____

○ _____

○ _____

WHAT TRIGGERED ME TODAY?

TODAY'S AFFIRMATION

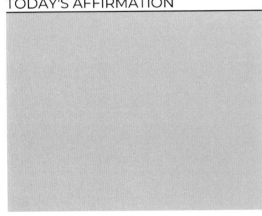

GOALS ACHEIVED TODAY

○ _____

○ _____

○ _____

○ _____

TODAY I FELT

WHAT I WANT TO REMEMBER ABOUT TODAY

SELF CARE FOR TODAY

EX: MEDITATE FOR 5 MINUTES

MY RANKING OF TODAY

Hi,

Thank you so much for purchasing The Think Better Feel Better journal. I designed this journal with the intention to promote self love, self care and mental health in women. I myself have dealt with many emotional traumas that have left me feeling weak, insecure, anxious, depressed and suicidal. It took me being at my lowest moment mentally for me to figure out that the change had to come from within. I was determined to save myself. The first thing I did was sign up for a therapist. This was life changing. All the skepticism I had went out the window. It felt great to have someone to share my thoughts with who didn't have a bias opinion about them. I then took time to isolate myself and dig deep into Lorrin, I needed to find out who she was. I couldn't believe I was 30 years old and couldn't answer basic self questions. Like what makes me happy. Isolation brought me clarity. My goals, intentions, bad habits, triggers and poor self talks all became very clear that they were the problem. My negative perception was filtering my life creating bad vibes and self inflicting trauma. All I had to do was shift my mind set. I began journaling, tracking my moods, digging into why I feel how I feel. I now have a much better perspective on life. I took the filter off and I am present, living my best life.

Made in the USA
Middletown, DE
08 January 2023

21682442R00055